This Church, These Times

The Roman Catholic Church
Since Vatican II

Artist   Franklin McMahon
Author   Francis X. Murphy
Foreword   Theodore Hesburgh

 Association Press
Follett Publishing Company/Chicago

Jacket and book design: Bob Sitkowski

Library of Congress Cataloging in Publication Data

McMahon, Franklin.
    This church, these times.

    1.   McMahon, Franklin.   2.   Catholic Church in art.
3.   Catholic Church—History—1965–   —Pictorial
works.   4.   Catholic Church—History—1965–   I.   Murphy, Francis Xavier, 1914–   II.   Title.
N6537.M336A4   1980   282′.09′047   80–15884
ISBN 0–695–81446–X
ISBN 0–695–81540–7 (pbk.)

First Printing

Contents

Foreword

Early evening in Bethlehem, the Holy Land.

I have known two Catholic churches in my lifetime. The church that I learned of at home, in school, in my parish, and, especially, in the seminary was a closed church—a church virtually without doubt, a church confident in its mode of governance and triumphalistic in its style of life.

The second Catholic church of my experience has been the postconciliar church. This is an open church—a church willing to listen as well as to pronounce, a church in which ministerial responsibility is shared, a church on pilgrimage.

The open church, despite the nostalgia of some for a more serene and settled past, is here to stay. The flow of history will not be reversed: no more lording it over other Christian communities; no more arrogance of "our" truth compared with "their" error; no more unconcern for a vast portion of a globe formerly labeled heathen or pagan; no more disdain for insights from a world in the past called profane; no more insensitivity to such immense problems as poverty, population, racism, and global injustice; no more cavalier treatment of the laity. A list such as this can caricature reality, but there is no item in it that does not have a history: that is why we had a Vatican Council II.

The postconciliar church is not more secure, more safe, more peaceful, or more orderly. But it is a better church—more Christlike and less worldly, and also less wealthy; more conscious of its central apostolic mission and how that relates to the poor and the powerless; more concerned with ecumenical "oneness in Christ" and less conscious about others finding us; more ready to serve the least in our society than to satisfy the comfortable; more interested in compassion than condemnation, praying for forgiveness for ourselves while pardoning all others.

But perhaps we are too close to our times to make definitive judgments. Let the chroniclers of the third millenium place the postconciliar church on their charts of the peaks and valleys attained over time by the People of God. Let us simply be grateful for the holy ones we are fortunate to have with us, the good leaders wherever they emerge, the great inspirations, the quiet heroes and heroines, and the high hopes and the roads leading to them.

This book, with its beautiful drawings by one of my favorite artists, Franklin McMahon, and the perceptive writing of a faithful student of Roman Catholic church affairs for many decades, Father Francis X. Murphy, C.SS.R., comes to us at a most propitious moment. It will serve to recall to our minds what has been and help us look forward to that which is to come through the work of the Spirit in the church—the People of God. Aided by the artistry of both Mr. McMahon and Father Murphy, all who care about what is happening in the church today and are curious about their own history will profit from a review of the recent events in the church during these significant past two decades.

Let us move ahead into the future with faith and hope and love, knowing that the church will somehow survive as it always has, as has been promised by the Lord Himself.

Rev. Theodore M. Hesburgh, C.S.C.
President
The University of Notre Dame

The University of Notre Dame.

Introduction

Castel Gandolfo is a small cliff-hanging town amid the *castelli romani* in the foothills overlooking Lake Albano, some eighteen miles south of Rome. Famed for its spacious view and salubrious air, the town is dominated by a picturesque medieval castle that has served as the summer residence of popes for centuries. There, on October 9, 1958, the aristocratic pontiff Pius XII breathed his last. His passing shocked the Catholic church's half billion faithful, its friends and its enemies all over the world. During his nineteen-year reign, Pius had achieved great prominence as a majestic figure, giving the papacy an aura of doctrinal omniscience and providing an example of political preciosity to a generation in turmoil.

Three weeks later the election of the portly, seventy-seven-year-old Cardinal Angelo Roncalli as John XXIII came as a surprise to both the world and to the eighty cardinals who, on the third day of the conclave, elected the aged patriarch of Venice pope. In his Oration for the Election of a Pontiff immediately preceding the conclave, Msgr. Antonio

Bacci had called for a pastoral instead of a political pope. He said that the new Holy Father should be a man intimately acquainted with the joys and sorrows of the faithful, and should stress the church's spiritual care for its people rather than pursue its involvement in worldly affairs.

To Bacci's amazement, within the first three months of his pontificate the peasant Holy Father from Sotto il Monte decided to do just that. He called for a coming together of the church's cardinals and bishops in an ecumenical council that would literally turn the Catholic church inside out.

As John confided to his secretary, Msgr. Loris Capovilla, he awoke one morning with Christ's command, "Go out into the whole world and preach my gospel to every creature," ringing in his ears. John suddenly realized that while the church was living in an age of instant communication, it was not achieving that objective; so he decided to hold a council. What he desired was an in-depth examination of the church's current situation—with its gains and losses, its faults and virtues—to discover just how its faithful were to present the good news of the gospel to the world in the latter half of the twentieth century.

As he informed a gathering of incredulous cardinals in late January 1959, John's objective was to update the church's teaching in such fashion that this ancient institution would prove itself capable of adapting its message to the "signs of the times." Despite the evangelical ring of that phrase, John's advisers considered his proposal rash, if not heretical. During the previous two hundred years, the papacy had strenuously opposed any such adaptation of its doctrine to the ephemeral spirit of the times. These men could see at once that such an adventitious assembly would challenge the conduct of the church at the top, thus calling into question current papal policies they considered sacrosanct and unchangeable. They realized that despite asking for an "updating"—John used the innocuous sounding word *aggiornamento*—rather than reform, John meant to introduce new ways of understanding the church's traditional teachings. As Cardinal Domenico Tardini, his secretary of state, told him bluntly, such a

13

gathering would bring about a revolution. To Tardini's consternation, John concurred in that irate prelate's prevision.

In the twenty years that separated the octogenarian pope, John XXIII—the peasant from Sotto il Monte—and the Polish pontiff, Carol Wojtyla—the poet and philosopher from Wadowice in the Tatra Mountains—the Catholic church suffered the reverberations of a recurring revolution. The origins of that revolution can be traced back two hundred years, to the refusal of the Roman pontiffs to confront their contemporary world with courage and determination. Instead, they adopted a policy of intransigence that destroyed the institution's credibility in the secular world while creating a ghetto mentality among a majority of its inhabitants. Nevertheless, the church universal seemed to prosper miraculously, pushing out in highly successful missionary adventures and surviving two world wars, attracting hundreds of thousands of converts while strengthening a regressive secular attitude among millions of its faithful in the well-to-do portions of the developed world.

As depicted here by the probing pencil and delicate brush of Franklin McMahon, the Roman Catholic church has experienced a total reorientation of its inner self-image over the past two decades, and a concomitant revision of its dealings with the outside world. In so doing, the church has acceded to the prompting of the Spirit under the aegis of four popes, each of whom imprinted his personal image on the papacy. Since exchanging Pius XII's majestic severity for John's pastoral benevolence, the papal office has experienced the troubled but patient guidance of Paul VI and the short-lived but revolutionary imprint of John Paul I. It is now in the hands of the enigmatic John Paul II. During the first year of his pontificate, the Polish pope, as a "man from afar," attained an aura of global recognition on a par with that of Pope John. But it seems that John Paul II has fallen back into what strikes many observers as a revival of the Pacelli pope's omnicompetence—an orientation eschewed by Vatican Council II as triumphalism.

Church leaders in Rome.

14

In the course of this brief survey of the church's revolutionary experience during the past two decades, special attention is paid to the people and movements that played an essential part in redrawing the dimensions of the church's structure and adapting its ancient teachings to the necessities of the twenty-first century. While critical in its objective, this essay means to reflect faithfully the excruciating travail that updating so venerable an institution invariably involves. To readers who may be disturbed by the author's occasional harsh judgments, he can only say that as one who played a very minor role in the unfolding of these events, he has called the shots as he has seen them. For whatever fault there may be in this viewpoint, he requests the reader's indulgence.

Father Francis X. Murphy
Washington, D.C.
May 1980

The monastery of Jasna Gora in Czestochowa, Poland.

I
John XXIII: A New Understanding

The opening ceremony at the Second Ecumenical Council in 1962 was four hours long. Pope John XXIII is shown at right.

With the unanticipated election of the portly septuagenarian Angelo Roncalli as John XXIII, the Catholic church was suddenly shaken to its foundations. John provided his generation with an explosive gathering of some 2,500 bishops and cardinals, to which he invited both other churchmen and the press as observers. On his mind was a reorientation of the way the church said its prayers, its understanding of the Scriptures, and its attitude toward the reunion of the Christian churches as well as its dealings with the outside world.

No sooner had Pope John announced his council than theologians and publicists poured out a plethora of books and articles giving a critical appraisal of the church's current status and offering directions for its updating. Of these critics, one of the most effective was the youthful Swiss theologian, Hans Küng, whose book *The Council, Reform and Reunion* became a best-seller. It called for a thorough reconsideration of the church's structures, the manner in which it explained its teaching, and a reform of the institution at all levels.

The council opened each day with mass. Protestant and Eastern Orthodox observers were seated next to the statue of St. Peter (at left) during the council sessions.

Küng's suggestions were a summation of concepts being aired by conscientious theologians since the close of World War II. These ideas had been expressed in such books as Yves Congar's *True and False Reform*, Bernard Häring's *The Law of Christ*, and Henri de Lubac's *Mystery of the Supernatural*, as well as in the writings of Karl Rahner, John Murray, M. D. Chenu, and Jean Daniélou. Nevertheless, Küng's book was criticized as an attack on the papacy. It was pilloried as a downgrading of Catholic teaching in Protestant fashion. Similar books and articles by the American Gustave Weigel, the Augustinian Gregory Baum, the anonymous Xavier Rynne, the journalist Robert Kaiser, and a flock of other correspondents were frowned upon by Vatican officials. They could only be bought in Rome's Catholic bookshops surreptitiously. But this suppressive effort merely added to their popularity.

As the council opened, two cardinals, Achille Liénart of Lille and Joseph Frings of Cologne, challenged the curia's selection of the council's working commissions—the bishops and theologians who would compose and correct the documents produced by the council. To their amazement, their challenge was upheld. This call for independence proved an excellent omen. It meant that John's inaugural speech, with its declaration of total freedom in the council's debates and its call for a thoroughgoing examination of the manner in which the church expressed its doctrines and discipline, would be honored.

In his opening speech John had said explicitly that the purpose of the council was not to discuss one or another of the church's traditional teachings but to so express them in a modern idiom that they would penetrate the consciousness and then the consciences of modern men and women. Characterizing many of his daily advisers as "prophets of doom who knew no history," he advised the council fathers that they were to adopt an optimistic outlook on the world and the church's ability to communicate its message of salvation.

In preparing for the council, John had distinguished between the curial officials, who were to carry on with their

21

daily tasks, and the members of the preparatory commissions. But under the shrewd management of his secretary of state, Cardinal Domenico Tardini, the two groups coalesced. This allowed the Vatican authorities to slow down the preparations and so overload the agenda for discussion that it appeared that it might be impossible to get the council off the ground.

Gradually, however, John activated a mild but positive propulsion. With the death of Cardinal Tardini in the summer of 1961, the pope brought in a great number of bishops and counselors from the universal church, who whipped the topics for debate into shape.

Nevertheless, these documents reflected a strictly traditionalist, textbook theology that would be rejected by a majority of the bishops. A general rule seemed to emerge requiring that these reactionary proposals be presented to the council as a stimulus to a thorough rethinking of their contents.

The prelates of the curia, abetted by some 250 bishops and religious superiors, constituted a *coetus patrum* ("gathering of the fathers") of traditionalists. They retained control of the workings of the conciliar debate through the secretary general, Archbishop Pericle Felici, and the assembly's president, the French cardinal, Eugene Tisserant. Nevertheless, a large proportion of the prelates from outside Rome were determined to implement Pope John's desires. They wanted to remake the church in such fashion that it could lead the Christian people to devote themselves to fulfilling Christ's injunction to feed the hungry, clothe the naked, educate the ignorant, and restore liberty to the oppressed.

These ecclesiastics included most of the residential cardinals from the north of Europe, among whom were Leo Suenens of Belgium; Bernard Alfrink of Holland; the successive cardinals of Paris, Feltin, Veuillot, and Marty; Julius Doepfner of Munich; Giacomo Lercaro of Bologna; and eventually, Michele Pellegrino of Turin. They were joined by Valerian Gracias of Bombay, Leon Duval of Algiers, and Peter Tatsuo Doi of Japan, with a cross section of Asian, African,

and Latin American prelates, including Juan Landazuri Ricketts of Lima, Raul Silva Henriquez of Chile, and Dom Heldar Pessoa Camara of Recife, Brazil.

Most of the English-speaking prelates—Cardinals Spellman of New York, Cushing of Boston, Ritter of St. Louis, Meyer of Chicago, Gilroy of Sydney, Conway of Ireland, and McCann of South Africa—proved to be somewhat confused in their attitude. They had been fully content with the preconciliar church and had a difficult time understanding John's vision of impending chaos. Their churches were filled each Sunday and holy day, their Catholic schools, from elementary to college, were overcrowded, the number of converts being brought into the church each year was overwhelming, and their finances were sound. In addition, they were supporting far-reaching missionary enterprises with vocations of priests and nuns, as well as with monetary assistance.

The English-speaking ecclesiastics also felt unhappy with the wide publicity given to the council's debates and disagreements in the public press and on radio and television. Nevertheless, they felt obliged to vote progressively when it came time to decide whether or not the Liturgy should be revised and updated to make it meaningful for contemporary Catholics in various parts of the world. They also agreed that the church was not a legal or juridical organization as it had been defined in the sixteenth century. Rather, it was a great mystery as described by Jesus Christ in the Gospels, where it consisted essentially of the "people of God."

Since it called itself catholic, the church had to reach out by redefining its attitude toward the handing down of the Sacred Scriptures, taking a realistic view of marriage and other social and political questions, as well as reviewing its approach to the other Christian churches. In so doing, it was bound to reconsider the structure of the church's hierarchy and the nature of the papal office.

An entirely new phenomenon in modern Catholic experience, Vatican Council II divided the church down the middle. On one side were the traditionalists who had been

Cardinal Peter Tatsuo Doi, archbishop of Tokyo.

24

Archbishop Thomas Roberts, S.J.

Archbishop Joseph Kiwanuka of Uganda.

Council participants continued discussions over coffee in St. Peter's. This coffee bar was nicknamed Bar Mitzvah; another was called Bar Jonah.

completely satisfied with the Pacellian church. Encouraged by their priests and bishops, mainly in the capitalist world, these Catholics had been content to attend mass in Latin on Sundays, to abstain from meat on Fridays and fast on the weekdays of Lent, to observe the fast from midnight before going to communion, to confess their sins weekly or at slightly greater intervals, and to contribute to the support not only of their pastors but of the church's missionaries all over the globe.

They had been exceedingly proud of Pope Pius XII, who, in his innumerable talks to learned societies and to the thousands of visitors who flocked to Rome, gave answers to contemporary social, economic, and political problems from a Catholic perspective. In addition, that pontiff's frequent appearances on radio and television gave the church an élan of catholicity more striking than that of any other religious institution.

In the late fifties and early sixties, these practicing Catholics felt that the church had never been better off. They, and their priests and prelates, simply could not understand this portly pope's determination to hold a council. Such an assembly, they felt, correctly, could only introduce discomfort and confusion.

On arriving in Rome for the council, the traditionalist bishops discovered that they had the support of the curial cardinals, from Ottaviani in the Holy Office to Amleto Cicognani as papal secretary of state. Cicognani, who for twenty-five years had been the apostolic delegate in Washington, had succeeded Tardini in that position after the latter's death in 1961. Though a man of great benevolence and far-reaching experience, Cicognani favored the conservative cause in the conciliar debates.

On the other side of the conciliar barrier was a group of cardinals and prelates, with their theologians, who accepted John's concern. They felt the need for change in the church's teaching methods and liturgical life so that the Christian people would become totally conscious of their primary task to love their neighbors as themselves. They agreed with the

Catholic publicist G. K. Chesterton, who rejected the claim that Christianity had been tried and found wanting. "It had been found difficult and not tried," Chesterton claimed.

The conciliar debate was conducted with propriety in the council's hall, each speaker being allotted ten minutes to put across his intervention in Latin. This linguistic rule was challenged by the intrepid Melkite patriarch, Maximos IV Saigh, who remarked that since Latin was not the *lingua franca* of the oriental churches, he would speak in French.

The fundamental thinking of the council was taking place in the commissions of bishops, theologians, and lay experts—with occasional assistance from non-Catholic observers—who were working on the drafts of the conciliar texts and documents. Equally busy and effective were the impromptu gatherings of prelates and *periti*, or experts, in hotel rooms and *pensioni*, where the finer points of the issues under debate were argued out, and short speeches were written for delivery by courageous prelates the following day.

The more influential of these clerical *botteghe scure*, or secluded dens, were frequented mainly by English-speaking experts, such as George Higgins and John Quinn of Chicago, Raymond Bosler of Indianapolis, Gregory Baum of Toronto, Mark Hurley of San Francisco, Peter Whitty of Liverpool, and William Baum, the future cardinal. The Tübingen theologian Hans Küng and the Redemptorist Bernard Häring were also frequently seen at the Chicago House of Santa Maria del Lago, the *pensione* Villanova near the Piazza Ungeria, and the Marist Generalate. And at the Jesuit headquarters on the Borgo Santo Spirito, mass was regularly concelebrated in the early evenings for journalists, lay observers, and visitors to the Eternal City.

For the second session of the council, a group of outstanding Catholic laymen and women joined the non-Catholic observers in the tribune of St. Andrew, immediately facing the main altar and the bank of presidents. Among these influential lay experts were the economist Barbara Ward and the assistant to the executive director of Catholic

Cardinal Albert Meyer, archbishop of Chicago, left Santa Maria del Lago each morning to attend council sessions. The villa was one of many where participants lived in Rome.

28

Cardinal Laurean Rugumbwa, bishop of Bukola, Tanzania, was the first African named a cardinal.

Relief Service, James Norris. Norris delivered an official Latin *relatio* of his own composition to introduce the debate on the church's involvement with the problem of world poverty. A close personal friend of Cardinal Montini before his elevation to the papacy, Norris had talked the Holy Father into allowing Barbara Ward to make that official presentation, but somewhere between the papal apartment and the council floor the plan was euchred, and Mr. Norris had to do the honors.

Also in the tribune were Jean Guitton, Vittorio Veronese, Federico Alessandrini, Rosemary Goldie, Pilar Belosillo, and representatives of the various Catholic lay organizations, from the Legion of Mary to the Opus Dei. They received occasional briefings from the gracious American Msgr. Luigi Ligutti, the Vatican observer at the Rome headquarters of the Food and Agriculture Organization of UNESCO, who exercised a powerful influence on the council's concern for the Third World.

One of the more colorful sights provided by the council was the arrival each morning of several dozen buses from the four corners of the city, out of which poured cardinals and bishops in their scarlet and red cassocks, oriental prelates in black and gold, and *periti* in soutanes, or in the brown, black, and white habits of their religious orders. Swinging briefcases like a group of schoolboys, they made hurried observations to colleagues entering the basilica or arranged dinner and other engagements.

A similar vignette greeted the sightseer in St. Peter's Square when, shortly before 1:00 P.M., these prelates poured out of the basilica headed for the buses that would take them to their respective hotels, *pensioni,* or religious houses for lunch and a well-merited siesta. In the late afternoon the more conscientious among them were seen hurrying to the unofficial lectures by *periti* in religious institutes or in the foyers of the U.S.O. and the crowded hotels in the shadow of the Vatican. They were waylaid by the press and radio and television correspondents for interviews or tidbits of inside information, or they enjoyed a few minutes of quiet while idling in the bookshops on the Via della Conciliazione leading to St. Peter's.

Immediately following the council Mass—celebrated in a different rite each morning—and the opening prayer led by Cardinal Tisserant, the secretary general sounded the *exeant omnes,* excluding all but the officially registered members of the council. Archbishop Felici then outlined the order of the debate and made other announcements pertaining to conciliar affairs.

The discussions began each morning with a handful of cardinals, each of whom approached the microphone text in hand. Their interventions absorbed the attention of the assembly in anticipation of someone taking an extreme position or making abrasive remarks, particularly if Cardinals Ernesto Ruffini of Palermo, John Carmel Heenan of Westminster, or Alfredo Ottaviani of the curia were in the lineup.

Among the more prominent of the English-speaking prelates were Cardinals Ritter of St. Louis, Meyer of Chicago, Shehan of Baltimore, and Spellman of New York. The talks of these cardinals were listened to with respect, as were the interventions of Archbishop Hallinan of Atlanta; Bishop Flahiff of Winnipeg; the Ukrainian Archbishop Maxim Hermaniuck; George Dwyer of Birmingham, England; Denis Hurley of Durban, South Africa; and Guilford Young of Tasmania.

Special attention was given to the prelates from behind the iron curtain, with particular deference to the cardinal of Warsaw, Stefan Wyszynski, and, after his release from custody, Cardinal Josef Beran of Prague. The latter's plea that the church take special note of the need for freedom of conscience and conviction in theological discussion made a great impression on the council. Beran connected many of the evils now being visited on the church by inimical regimes with the church's severity in the past. He gave particular attention to the burning at the stake of John Hus, the fifteenth-century Czech reformer, despite the guarantee of safety Hus had received before attending the Council of Constance.

Seated in a balcony overlooking the council sessions were the periti—*those theologians, liturgists, and canon lawyers who served as advisers to delegates.*

Delegate votes were tabulated on a computer housed in a room below the statue of Pope Gregory XVI.

Msgr. George Higgins of Washington, D.C.

Three American bishops at the council were
Archbishop Dearden of Detroit, Cardinal Shehan
of Baltimore, and Bishop Wright of Pittsburgh.

Antiwar activists Archbishop Thomas Roberts, Richard Carbray, and Eileen Egan discussed their hopes for a council statement on conscientious objection while dining in a Rome restaurant.

The major archbishop of the Ukraine, Josef Slipyi, was also welcomed with great respect. Slipyi was released from imprisonment in Siberia as a gesture of benevolence on the part of Khrushchev for Pope John. Created a cardinal, Slipyi wanted to be recognized as the patriarch of the Ukrainian rite—an impossible arrangement, for it would have ostensibly given him jurisdiction over Ukrainian Catholics all over the world. This gesture would have constituted an obstacle to all future relations between the Vatican and Moscow and other orthodox patriarchates. In the early seventies, Slipyi was to maintain that he suffered more during his eighteen years of freedom in Rome than during his incarceration in Russian prisons.

Years later, Pope Paul would have a similar difficulty with Cardinal Jozsef Mindszenty of Hungary. Mindszenty had suffered a humiliating public trial after being brainwashed by the Communists in 1948. After the Hungarian uprising of 1956, he took refuge in the American Embassy in Budapest. He refused all invitations to leave his asylum until 1970, when Pope Paul finally persuaded him to take up residence in Vienna after a triumphal visit to Rome. Two years later, Paul had to deprive him of his title as archbishop of Esztergom in order to reach an agreement with the Hungarian government over the appointment of bishops. The aggrieved confessor of the faith made a loud protest, taking his complaint to the American public, but Mindszenty was mercifully removed from the scene by death a few months later.

Pope John's council began amid considerable confusion. Only at the last moment did the Holy Father decide to initiate the debate with a discussion of the Liturgy—the way the church said its prayers. The document prepared for the council was a long, unwieldy curial statement. The Holy Father felt that it would be quickly cast aside and that the conciliar fathers would then work out the main issues by updating the ceremonies of the Mass and the Sacraments, authorizing the use of the vernacular languages in the western rite, and encouraging the intimate participation of the laity in the church's official prayer life.

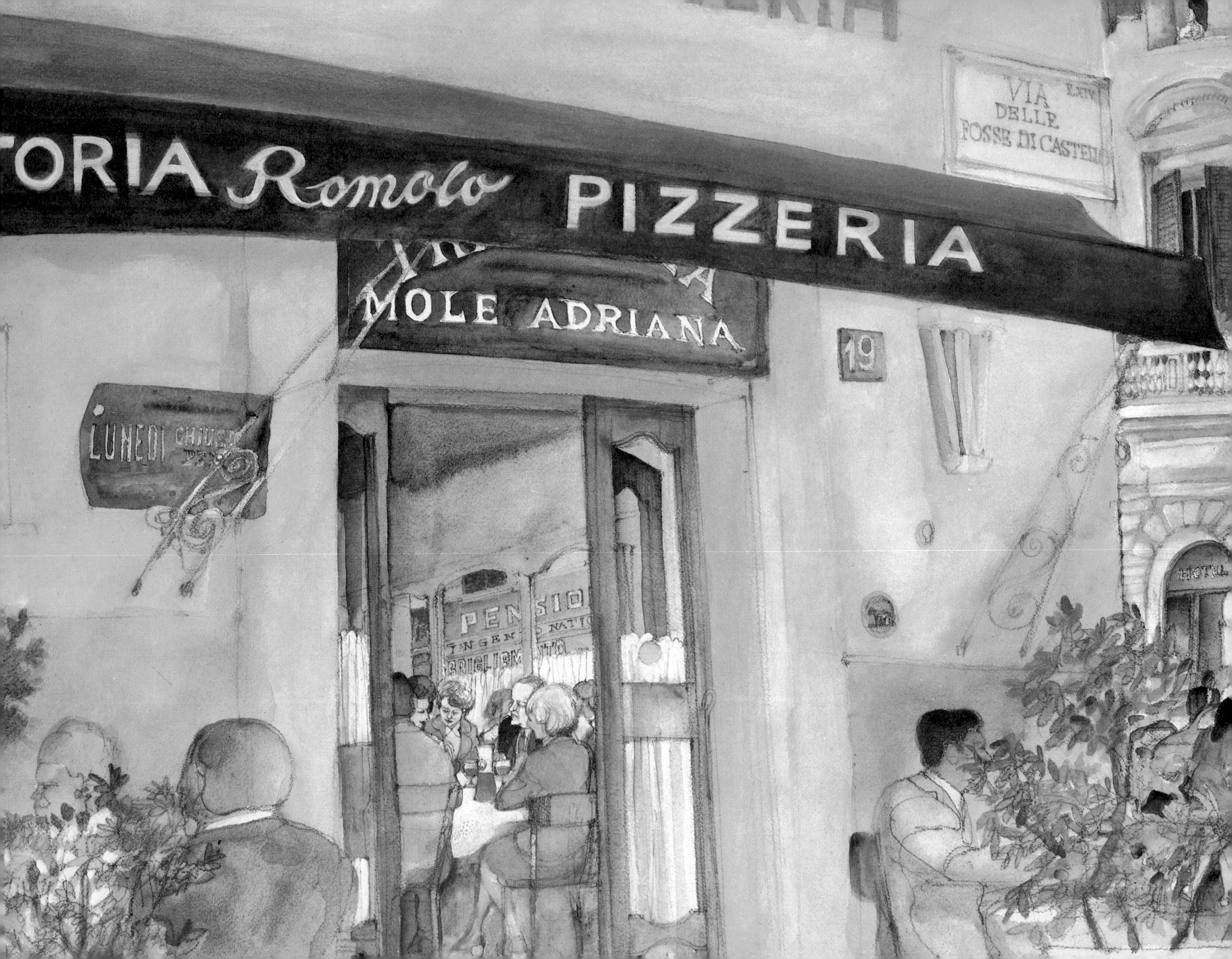
TORIA Romolo
PIZZERIA
MOLE ADRIANA
VIA
DELLE
19
LUNEDI

Patrick and Patty Crowley, founders of the Christian Family Movement, met in a Rome cafe to talk about their interest in council debates.

Protestant and Orthodox observers gather before a session of the council.

Mother Mary Luke from the United States was the first woman observer named to the council.

Instead of a brief discussion, the debate was elongated with an intricate argument illustrating the pertinence of the ancient theological axiom, *Lex orandi, lex credendi*—the church's prayer reflects its belief. Prelates lined up quickly on either side of the traditionalist vs. progressive argument that was to characterize hard-fought positions during all four sessions. The debate was to reach heights and depths of disagreement that shocked both members of the council and the outside world.

It soon became apparent that a majority favored John's call for an updating. Among these progressives, however, there was sufficient hesitation and uncertainty to allow the opposition to get the advantage. This was illustrated by a crucial vote on the schema on divine revelation. John had to intervene personally to remove the preparatory document from debate even though it did not receive a two-thirds majority vote for rejection. He entrusted the construction of a new document to a mixed commission under Cardinals Ottaviani and Agostino Bea. The latter was an eighty-two-year-old Jesuit, a former Scripture professor who had suddenly turned futuristic in his loyalties. Bea was able to usher through the council both a progressive agreement on the nature of Scripture in relation to tradition and the all-important declaration on religious liberty.

Meanwhile, John's popularity as a world leader had grown by leaps and bounds. In bringing the first session of the council to an end in late 1962, he admitted that this opening round of debate lacked direction and precision. So he entrusted preparation of the next round to Cardinals Suenens and Montini. They divided the work into a discussion of the church *ad intra* ("from within itself") and *ad extra* ("in relation to the outside world"). John then instructed the bishops to do their homework conscientiously and "in silence"—a mischievous reference to the clamor of the debate. They were to reassemble in Rome on September 8 the following year.

In the interim, John turned out two encyclicals, *Mater et Magistra* (the church as "Mother and Teacher") and *Pacem in Terris* ("Peace on Earth") that were to serve, along with his

opening talk at the council, as the magna charta of the church in the new age. In all these documents John insisted that while the church had acted with severity in the past, that attitude was no longer necessary. What was needed was a statement of Christian truths that would affect the consciousness and eventually the consciences of contemporary men and women.

In the spring of 1962, a confrontation developed between John Kennedy and Nikita Khrushchev over the implantation of nuclear missiles in Cuba. As the tension mounted, Pope John suddenly appeared on television in a plea to the two leaders to keep the peace. To his amazement, as he confided to an aide, these people listened when he talked. Khrushchev and Kennedy backed down. John set Msgr. Pietro Pavan, one of his trusted noncurial aides, to prepare the basis for an encyclical on peace. In this document he made the famous distinction between communism as an atheist ideology that had to be repudiated, and as a political system seeking justice in the social and economic order that could be tolerated. At the suggestion of U Thant, John sent Cardinal Suenens of Belgium to be his official representative in presenting a copy of *Pacem in Terris* to the United Nations. The encyclical was used as the basis for a series of symposia involving world leaders in a down-to-earth discussion of peace on earth.

With the acquiescence of the Soviet leader, whose daughter and son-in-law John had entertained in a private audience in the Vatican (giving the lady a rosary and a special message for her father), John received the Balzan Peace Prize. On that occasion he made an official visit to the Quirinal Palace, the ancient home of the popes but since 1870 the headquarters of first the king and then the president of Italy. It was his last public appearance. Several weeks later, during the first days of June, the whole world seemed to be involved in his final agony—a devout and dignified experience that was reported as "a death in the family of mankind."

Death of Pope John XXIII.

II
Paul VI: Between the Old and the New

Council sessions continued during the first two years of Pope Paul VI's pontificate. The painting here was done during the vote on "The Declaration on the Relation of the Church to Non-Christian Religions."

In the conclave that followed John's death, a struggle ensued between the conservative papal electors who favored the candidacy of the curial cardinal, Ildebrando Antoniutti, and the progressives who supported the cardinal of Milan, Giovanni Battista Montini—known as John's *delfino,* or protege. Montini would certainly continue the council; he had said as much in the funeral oration he preached for John in his cathedral of Milan.

Antoniutti was a tall, aristocratic figure who had occupied high diplomatic posts in Canada and Madrid and was known to favor both the Franco regime and the Opus Dei. The latter was a secular religious institute begun in Spain that included both clergy and married and single laity and sought to involve its members in influential positions in the academic, business, and political spheres. This severely conservative organization was barely conciliar in its policies. They reflected the ideas of Cardinal Antoniutti from Udine.

Montini was a Brescian whose father had played a leading role in Vatican affairs as banker, agricultural entrepreneur,

journalist, and politician. Ordained a priest in 1921,
young Giovanni Montini registered for literature at the University of Rome but was soon ensconced in the college of
ecclesiastical nobles and prepared for a curial career by Msgr.
Guiseppe Pizzardo. While serving as a *minutante*, or clerk, in
the Vatican, Montini also worked with the future cardinal
Amleto Cicognani as a chaplain to university students. He
eventually served under two imperious popes, Pius XI and
Pius XII, as *sostituto*, or man of confidence, in the secretariat
of state. In late 1954, however, he was ushered out of the
Vatican and made archbishop of Milan but not given the cardinal's hat that for centuries went with that prime archbishopric. His crime was the support he had given to the
Christian Democratic leader Alcide de Gasperi's desire to
oust the Vatican from Italian politics.

In Milan, Montini immediately received the support of
the fatherly patriarch of Venice, Angelo Roncalli. When the
latter became pope, Montini was his first creation as cardinal.
He resided in the Vatican during the first session of the
council, and, with Cardinal Suenens of Belgium, was John's
most trusted collaborator.

Elected pope on June 23, 1963, Montini immediately announced his intention of continuing the council. He set its
opening session for September 28. He likewise appointed
four cardinals as moderators to control the debate: Suenens,
Lercaro of Bologna, Doepfner of Munich, and the Armenian
Gregory Agagianian.

Over the course of the next three years, Paul displayed
heroic sufferance—not merely in keeping the council together but in shepherding its sixteen documents to a successful promulgation with the words "It seemed good to the
Holy Spirit and to us. . . ." He likewise began a series of ten
jet voyages with a December 1963 trip to Jerusalem, where
he met the Orthodox Greek patriarch, Athenagoras, with the
kiss of peace after nine hundred years of enmity between
the two churches. Pope Paul visited India, Africa, Turkey,
Portugal, Geneva, and the United Nations in New York; sat
in on the inauguration of the Medellín Conference of Latin

Pope Paul celebrated mass in the Grotto of the Church of the Nativity in Bethlehem during his visit to the Holy Land.

In Jerusalem, the pope walked along the Via Dolorosa.

Pope Paul celebrated mass in Yankee Stadium during his New York visit.

In an address to the General Assembly of the United Nations in 1965, Pope Paul pleaded for peace.

American Bishops in Bogotá; and then embarked on a voyage halfway round the world to the Philippines, Indonesia, Samoa, and Australia. On all these journeys, Paul was accompanied by the tall, powerful Chicagoan, Bishop Paul Marcinkus, who worked out his itinerary and acted as the pope's aide and bodyguard.

Before the General Assembly of the United Nations on October 4, 1965, the Holy Father gave an impassioned message of peace, crying "War no more! War never again!" And in Bogotá he confirmed the message of his 1967 encyclical *Populorum Progressio* ("On the Development of Peoples") condemning governments guilty of the oppression of their people and justifying the church's total involvement with the poor and the oppressed.

Shortly before the council's close in December 1965, Paul had taken to heart John's distinction between the "truths of the faith" and "how they are expressed." He thus abolished the old Holy Office with its Inquisition and Index of Forbidden Books. In its place he set up the Congregation for the Doctrine of the Faith, giving this office the positive aim of promoting forward-looking theological investigation rather than persecuting the church's more adventuresome thinkers. But he failed to change the personnel, who doggedly kept their old ways of riding herd on the church's theologians. Likewise at the council's close, Pope Paul was persuaded to call a *vacatio legis*, or moratorium, a holding off of the conciliar decrees and constitutions until the curia could issue official interpretations of these documents.

A council document is the end result of a great debate aimed at achieving a consensus among a large majority of the church's prelates; it summarizes the church's tradition as of the day it is promulgated. It then leaves an opening for what John had termed *un balzo in avanti* ("a leap ahead"). Read from a 1955 viewpoint, the document could justify the most recalcitrant refusal to update church teaching. Read from the vantage point of 1975, the constitutions and decrees justify a complete revision of doctrinal expression and disciplinary structure.

In attempting to postpone the implementation of the council's directives, the curial strategy proved fatal as far as papal authority was concerned. Zealous apostles and committed Catholics had been reading and absorbing the council's achievements, and they could see no reason for holding back the reforms sanctioned by the council fathers and promulgated with the approbation of the Holy Spirit.

In the ensuing struggle between recalcitrant bishops and the younger generation of priests, nuns, and brothers, the doors of rectories and convents flew open, and clerics and sisters by the thousands abandoned their vocations. Most of them had been shocked by the Vatican's refusal to obey the obvious promptings of the Holy Spirit. Hence they decided to seek new situations. A majority of both priests and nuns remained within the church's structure, seeking laicization and permission to marry. A few lost their faith along with their original calling. Overwhelmed at first by this incredible loss, Pope Paul reacted in anger. But then, with benevolent resignation, he granted some 30,000 dispensations from priestly vows, allowing the petitioners to marry.

Early in 1968, Pope Paul published his *Credo* of the Christian people. It proved to be a not very successful restatement of Catholic belief. Then, in late July, he brought upon himself and the church a violent reaction that still bothers the faithful and a concerned public who have some feeling for the church's effect on world opinion.

With the publication of his encyclical, *Humanae Vitae* ("On Human Life"), Pope Paul sealed his fate in the popular estimation as essentially a backward-looking pope. Rejecting the advice of both a theologico-scientific advisory group and a commission of cardinals who advised him to change church teaching in the matter, Paul condemned the use of artificial contraceptives as sinful. By asserting that "every conjugal act must be open to the transmission of life," the pope seemed to be returning to a biological basis for determining the essence of a moral judgment. But the council had stated plainly that the morality of an action should be based upon the nature of man and his activities. The pope was relying on what

Pope John's encyclical Pacem in Terris *sparked many international gatherings of world leaders to discuss the foundations for world peace. Among those participating during a meeting in 1973 were Hubert Humphrey and George McGovern.*

Vatican Council pronouncements encouraged the participation of priests and nuns in the civil rights movement in America. Many marched with Dr. Martin Luther King, Jr., in the 1965 demonstrations in Selma, Alabama.

he considered a "natural law" built into man's makeup, while the council was basing its evaluation on the human being's rational and spiritual nature.

In the reaction to the encyclical, papal authority—an area in which Paul was highly sensitive—was challenged by groups of younger parish priests and theologians. Here and there misguided prelates—in Washington, D.C. and in Southwark, England—made an issue of what they considered rebellion and drove a number of conscientious clerics out of the priesthood. But the pope took no such action. Nor did he exhibit great displeasure when the episcopal conferences of Holland, Belgium, Scandinavia, Mexico, Germany, Indonesia, and Canada interpreted the papal decision in a highly benevolent fashion.

The French bishops, under the guidance of Father Martelet, one of Paul's chief advisers, said that while a contraceptive act was always a disorder, it need not be a sin. And the Italian episcopate, while praising the encyclical as a high ideal, told their people that if they did not reach that ideal they need not consider themselves in sin.

Most of the English-speaking episcopates bowed their heads unfeelingly beneath the papal ban. And when the United States bishops agreed that each couple had a right to follow its conscience in making a decision, John Wright, the future curial cardinal, told them that only a conscience based on the papal decision could be trusted.

In the world outside the church, the encyclical was viewed as a disaster by those concerned with the problems of overpopulation. But with time, it came to be seen as a *felix culpa*, a fortunate error, that finally forced the United Nations to take a thorough look at the problem of birth control on a worldwide scale, leading to the Population Year 1974.

In accepting the papal office in June 1963, Paul had every intention of reforming the curia. He told its members that they were administrative officials, not policymakers. But a delicacy in not wanting to be considered vindictive prevented him from ridding these offices of their bureaucratic officials, many of whom had been part of the conspiracy that caused his removal from the Vatican in 1954. He did break with the old "black" Italian aristocracy—the families of former popes—telling them there was nothing he could do for them.

Then in 1967 he published *De Regimini Ecclesiae* ("On the Government of the Church"), which was meant to give the curial offices a new orientation as members of the papal household.

Nevertheless, by again failing to immediately remove the older officials and personnel, the reform proved a matter of nominal rather than basic change. Late that year, with the aid of his former secretary, Archbishop Benelli, Paul set about retiring a group of ancient cardinals—Ottaviani, Testa, and Larraona. He replaced them with an international group that included the Frenchman Gabriel Garrone, the American John Wright, the Yugoslav Franjo Seper, and the Belgian Maximilian De Furstenberg—all of whom quickly proved themselves to be more Italian than the Italians.

In his appointment of cardinals and bishops, Paul showed himself conscious of the need for a good balance of conservative and progressive prelates in the church's leadership, a policy not always followed by his curial-dominated nuncios and apostolic delegates.

In 1967, Paul inaugurated the Roman Synod of Bishops, a triennial gathering of delegates elected by their national conferences of bishops. He invited them to sit down with the curial cardinals to discuss important matters of church policy. In a series of month-long sessions in 1967, 1971, 1974, and 1977, they dealt with topics that included the priestly ministry and the nature of ecclesiastical authority, as well as the means of evangelization and catechesis in today's world.

On an African visit to Uganda in 1969, Paul said that the church on that continent was in need of Africanization. But in the synod of 1974, he reneged on the pluralism in doctrinal expression and discipline that that policy encouraged. Nevertheless, under his auspices, the church seemed to leap ahead in mission territories, where, despite revolutions and

The Most Reverend James Shannon from St. Paul, the ranking Roman Catholic prelate at the Selma march, spoke in Brown Chapel. Beside him was Archbishop Iakovos of the Greek Orthodox church.

Dr. King's supporters gathered in the basement of the First Baptist Church in Selma to plan their protests against racial prejudice.

58

When Dr. King brought the civil rights movement north to Chicago, religious and civic leaders met to struggle with the issue of justice for black people. Above, John McDermott led meetings of the Catholic Interracial Council.

Edward Marciniak met with members of his Chicago Commission on Human Relations.

political oppression, he was able to install dozens of native bishops.

In his Ostpolitik Paul employed Msgr. Agostino Casaroli, whom Pope John had previously sent behind the iron curtain to arrange a détente between the church and the Communist leaders. Pope Paul was the first to applaud President Nixon's trip to continental China in 1971 and made a great effort to open relations with the Mao Tse-tung regime, where some two or three million Catholics and as many more Christians were known to be living clandestinely.

With the thaw in China's religious orientation that followed the death of Mao, the pope gravely offended Cardinal Yu Pin of Taiwan by removing the papal nuncio from Taipei as a gesture of goodwill toward continental China. But as priest-journalist Louis Wei argued, the papal concern for two million persecuted Catholics behind the bamboo curtain should outweigh political relations with a land harboring some 200,000 well-cared-for Catholics.

During the year of rebellion 1968, Pope Paul kept a watchful eye on Catholic involvement in the universities and other institutions whose social philosophies and political policies were being challenged. He kept the curia out of such local situations as those created by the Berrigan brothers and the Catonsville 9, with their well-publicized defiance of the public authorities in opposition to the war in Vietnam. And the pontiff approved the benevolent handling of these priests in prison by the cardinal of Baltimore, Lawrence Shehan, despite complaints to the Holy See about the scandal. Actually, Paul had chided President Lyndon Johnson, to that proud man's great annoyance, over the continuation of the Vietnam war when he received the American leader in audience just before Christmas 1967.

Paul kept himself well informed concerning the Catholic participation in ecumenical movements to achieve social justice for blacks in both the northern and southern sections of the United States, praising the efforts of the Protestant pastor Martin Luther King, Jr. He also supported courageous bishops and people defying the local governments in South

Africa and Rhodesia. Paul appreciated the work of Msgr. George Higgins and a number of bishops in the United States who gave full support to the efforts of such dedicated leaders as Cesar Chavez to obtain justice and decent living conditions for migrant Chicano farmworkers. And he demonstrated an interest in such spiritual endeavors as the Cursillo movement, which made so salutary an impression on American Catholicism.

In 1970 Paul circled the globe from Hong Kong and the Philippines to Indonesia, Samoa, and Australia. Immediately before leaving Rome, he issued a decree depriving cardinals of a vote in a papal conclave once they reached their eightieth birthdays. Forced to retire from their offices, such octogenarian cardinals as Ottaviani and Tisserant—both with vows of obedience to the pontiff—put up a clamor that was loud and long. But the pope held to his decision. Then, on his own eightieth birthday, Pope Paul had to evade their suggestions that he obey his own rule by letting it be known that "the father of the family does not retire."

In June 1977 Paul created four cardinals. Conscious of the embarrassing situation in which he had been placed on leaving the Vatican in 1954, he made a cardinal of the *sostituto*, Msgr. Giovanni Benelli, dispatching him to Florence as its new archbishop. Suffering from a painful arthrosis in his legs and hip, the pontiff kept on the move, making frequent and cheerful references to his impending dissolution. In a sermon some time before his death, he said that old age brought many inconveniences—one of which was, of course, the end. He had the good fortune to retain his faculties down to the moment before he died, on Sunday, August 6, 1978. He had been at work the previous day with a public audience to a large crowd at Castel Gandolfo.

In his will the pontiff requested that his obsequies be conducted with the utmost simplicity and that he be buried deep in the earth close to the tombs of Pope John and St. Peter. In keeping with his wishes, his unadorned wooden coffin was placed on a rug above the cobblestones of the *sagrata* in St. Peter's Square. Adorned with a book of the

Leaders of the Catholic antiwar movement in America were Father Daniel Berrigan (above) and his brother, Father Philip Berrigan.

Pope Paul VI inaugurated the Roman Synod of Bishops to help with the governance of the church. The first synod met in a catacomblike room deep in St. Peter's Basilica in 1967. Others were held until 1977, the year before the pope's death.

Gospels, it lay in front of a large rectangular altar at which a hundred cardinals in the dark red chasubles of papal mourning celebrated a Mass of the Resurrection. At the ceremony's conclusion the simple box was hoisted on the shoulders of papal functionaries and slowly marched up the *scalinata* leading into the darkened basilica. A wave of muffled applause spread across the immense crowd. It was a final tribute to a pontiff whose troubled reign had finally found its *raison d'être* in the totally Christian atmosphere that surrounded his death and burial.

III
John Paul I: A Simple Beginning

The death of Pope Paul caught the church and the Roman curia by surprise. Most of the cardinals had left Rome for their August holidays, and some had difficulty returning at once for the papal obsequies and the twice-a-day cardinalitial meetings during which they governed the church. At the death of the pope, all the officials of the papal household lost their positions. A caretaker government under the *camerlengo*, Cardinal Jean Villot, Paul's secretary of state, and the body of cardinals made decisions governing the coming conclave and the church's daily needs.

During the three weeks following Paul's demise, speculation in the media regarding the *papabili*, or candidates for the papacy, took on the aspects of a political campaign that, paradoxically, lacked the cooperation of its principals. Nevertheless, while politicking as such was forbidden, there were private meetings of the cardinals over dinner and in special gatherings, during which the needs of the church were outlined and the character of the cardinal who seemed best fitted for the papacy was discussed.

67

During the conclave the first ballot gave seventy-two-year-old Cardinal Giuseppe Siri of Genoa, the favorite of the conservatives, a small lead over the patriarch of Venice, Albino Luciani. On the second ballot Siri and Luciani each gained proportionately. The electors then looked closely at Luciani, an unpretentious prelate with an engaging smile and a reputation as a serious thinker and literary wit.

During the third ballot, as the new pope himself revealed the next day, Luciani suddenly saw "a great danger" coming close to him. He had to be comforted by the cardinals on his right and left, Willebrands of Utrecht and Ribeiro of Lisbon. His support grew to over 60 votes; then, on the fourth ballot, he was elected, with over 90 of the 111 votes.

Appearing before the expectant crowds, on the balcony above the entrance to the basilica, the new pontiff seemed uncomfortable in his hastily fitted white cassock and zucchetto. But with his joyous face and pleasant voice, he delighted the audience in the square below and throughout the world as he gave his blessing *urbi et orbi* ("to the city and to the world").

How well the new pontiff slept that night is not known. But the next day, in his noonday appearance on the balcony of St. Peter's to say the Angelus to an immense crowd of visitors, the pope endeared himself to them. *"Ieri,"* ("Yesterday") he began, and immediately the crowd in the piazza caught the fact that the pope was about to indulge in an indiscretion. As he repeated *"Ieri,"* they burst into loud and prolonged laughter, sharing the pope's own enjoyment of the situation.

Finally regaining his composure, John Paul confessed to having been serene and unperturbed as he entered the Sistine Chapel to vote the previous day. Then, suddenly, he saw the danger nearing him. But despite his fears, when the offer came, he accepted it. Now he wanted the world to know that he would carry out the desires of both Pope John and Pope Paul, whose names he had assumed. He would do so in true collegial fashion, with the aid of the bishops.

The new pope took one major decision without consulting his senior advisers. He had himself installed as the bishop of Rome by the mere placing over his shoulders of the pallium—the two-inch wide, square stole of white lamb's wool that had been the sign of metropolitan authority in the church from the earliest times. It was a significant act of humility that changed a thousand-year tradition. Then, with the cardinals, he concelebrated a mass in St. Peter's Square before a multitude of visitors, including kings, diplomats, heads of state, and representatives of other religions.

John Paul spent his first and only month as the church's supreme pastor (he did not want to be called a pontiff) learning the ropes of papal government. Then he was gone. Retiring to his quarters shortly after ten on a Thursday evening, he did not appear for mass at 5:30 the following morning. Alarmed at this unusual occurrence, the pope's secretary, Fr. John Magee, entered his room to discover him dead in bed. The Luciani pope had died of a massive heart attack about 11:00 P.M., while reading the text of a talk he was to give the next day.

John Paul's obsequies, like those for his predecessor, were conducted in the open square in front of St. Peter's with a simple wooden casket on the *sagrato* before the large rectangular altar. Led by the aristocratic cardinal, Carlo Confalonieri, about a hundred cardinals in the dark red of papal mourning concelebrated mass in the pelting rain. Despite the inclement weather, the piazza was crowded with the umbrella-covered faithful, diplomats, and ecclesiastics. Once more, as the coffin was raised to the shoulders of the Vatican retainers, a wave of applause accompanied the slow march into the basilica. John Paul I was no more.

IV
John Paul II: A Mission to the World

Pope John Paul II's first trip abroad as pope was to Mexico to attend the CELAM III (Consejo Episcopal Latino-americano) conference of Latin American bishops. While in Mexico, he celebrated mass before the Altar of the Kings in the Cathedral of Mexico, the oldest and largest in Latin America.

Following the death of the Luciani pope, the apparatus for conducting the church's affairs during the *sede vacante* was put into motion once again by the papal *camerlengo*, Cardinal Jean Villot. The 111 eligible cardinal electors were summoned to Rome posthaste. Among them, the fifty-eight-year-old cardinal of Krakow, Carol Wojtyla, seemed particularly disturbed by the news of John Paul's demise. According to his housekeeper, on hearing of Pope Paul's death in August, Wojtyla had taken that news in stride, making the rounds of leave-taking of his entourage before departing for Rome. This time, he simply disappeared. Upon arriving in Rome he set out for the mountain shrine of Montereale, where he spent four days in retreat. On his return to the Vatican he seemed completely at ease, participating regularly in the cardinals' meetings.

Preparations for the new conclave were expedited and October 14 was set for the entrance into the Sistine area. The precautions for secrecy were greatly modified, giving the electors space for breathing. The cardinals entered the area of

73

the conclave on Saturday evening well prepared for the role they were to play. Once again, despite vigorous discussions in the press and communications media, and a few minor political incidents, absolutely nothing was known of the mind of the electors.

The voting began at nine on Sunday morning. At eleven and again toward seven o'clock that evening black smoke poured from the Sistine chimney. Again at eleven the next day, the puffs of smoke were nowhere near white. But at 6:18 that Monday evening, the cry *"E bianco! E bianco!"* ("It's white! It's white!") suddenly echoed over the vast piazza and throughout the world. Again, in what could only be considered a fateful experience, within two days, and on the eighth ballot, the cardinals had produced a new Holy Father. And when his identity was revealed, it caught the church and the world by surprise. After 455 years of Italian dominance in the papacy, the Holy See now had a man from afar, a Polish bishop of Rome. What was more, he was a comparatively young man, of great physical strength, with an open face and wide blue eyes.

Carol Wojtyla, the cardinal of Krakow, was known as a poet and philosopher, a world traveler, a ski buff, and a nature lover. Only a month before, he had gone on a canoe jaunt with university students in his native Tatra Mountains. All this information came dribbling out on television and radio following the first shock of the Vatican announcement.

When the new Holy Father appeared to give his blessing, he cast protocol aside. Grasping the balustrade of the balcony over St. Peter's Basilica with his two large hands, he cried out, *"Sia lodato Gesu Christo!"* ("Let Jesus Christ be praised!")

To their own consternation, a majority of Italians and clerics in the piazza heard themselves answering, *"Sia sempre lodato!"* ("May he always be praised!"), an ancient salutation within the church that had, over the past twenty years, fallen into disuse. Immediately afterward, John Paul II announced that although he was "a man from afar," he was now the

Crowds awaited the coming of the pope to their community in Mexico. On the following two pages are paintings of crowds at the Cathedral of Mexico in Mexico City and of the pope as he celebrated mass in the modern Basilica of Our Lady of Guadalupe outside the city.

bishop of Rome and would do his best to speak "your—no—our language." With that he had won the Italian populace. When he continued by announcing that with his pontificate he intended to open a new path in history, he won over the rest of the world.

John Paul II had himself installed in the same manner as his immediate predecessor, with the simple ceremony of the pallium and the concelebrated mass in St. Peter's Square. These festivities had been moved to the early morning in order not to interfere with a champion football match that would absorb the attention of the Italians that afternoon.

More formal than the Luciani pope in his public addresses, John Paul II proved totally people-conscious in granting audiences to the diplomats, ecclesiastics, and journalists. He waded in among these people to enjoy direct contact with the crowds, as if he were running for political office. His address to the world on the following morning was a more personal effort than his predecessor's, though it repeated the same objectives—to get on with the prosecution of John's and Paul's programs as outlined by the council and to involve the church in the great search for peace and stability needed by the contemporary world.

Among the questions put to the pope personally by the journalists in the great hall of benedictions were "Will you come to Ireland?" "Will you visit Russia?" "Do you intend to return home to Poland?" and "What about the Puebla meeting in Mexico?" To all these queries he replied, "Yes, if they let me!"

Educated in his native Krakow—he had been born in Wadowice on May 18, 1920, and orphaned after reaching eighteen—Wojtyla had spent the war in the archbishop's palace aiding Cardinal Sapieha in his refugee endeavors and studying theology. Ordained a priest in 1946, he spent two years at the Dominican-run Angelicum in Rome, pursuing theological studies and caring for refugee Poles in France, Germany, and Belgium. On his return to Krakow, he taught courses in moral values to university students, produced a respectable portfolio of his own writings, and exhibited a flair for poetry.

Hundreds of people waited all night for the coming of the pope to Puebla, Mexico, where the CELAM III conference was held.

*Pope John Paul II arrived in a motorcade
the next day.*

BIENVENIDO

Consecrated auxiliary bishop of Krakow in 1958, Wojtyla became an archbishop in 1964 and a cardinal in 1967. He had attended all four sessions of Vatican Council II as a working theologian as well as the triennial assemblies of the Roman Synod of Bishops as a member of its permanent staff. He had also done considerable traveling in the United States, Canada, and Brazil, and had taken a trip halfway round the world to Indonesia and Australia delivering philosophical lectures. Thus, his qualifications to lead the church universal were impressive as he took on the mysterious task of serving as the 265th successor to Peter as bishop of Rome.

The election itself had been a strongly contested battle on the first day between the septuagenarian Cardinal Siri of Genoa, strangely supported once more by the curial faction, and the youthful cardinal of Florence, Giovanni Benelli, with Pericle Felici an interesting third candidate bringing up the rear. On the third ballot, on Sunday afternoon, Benelli rose to some fifty or fifty-five votes, twenty short of the necessary two-thirds plus one needed for election. He had peaked, and on the next ballot, there was a scattering of votes for the older Italian residential cardinals such as Ursi of Naples and Colombo of Milan.

After dinner that evening it became clear that if the Italians and their supporters could not agree on a candidate the next morning, the conclave would look elsewhere.

Meanwhile, Wojtyla's name had sounded sporadically in the voting; Cardinal Koenig of Vienna later admitted that Wojtyla had been his candidate from the start. It was during the luncheon break on Monday that the cardinal of Krakow's fate was sealed when the electors got a good look at him and discovered his exceptional background. As Cardinal Hume of Britain would remark later, "We would have voted for him even if he were an Italian."

On the seventh ballot, Wojtyla's name suddenly shot toward the top, and he was in on the eighth. As he confessed in his first encyclical, his thoughts on accepting the papal office were trained on Christ the Redeemer. Impressed by the simple magnanimity of his immediate, short-lived

Impromptu press conferences were held at Palafox Seminary, site of the CELAM III meetings.

81

CELAM III meetings.

predecessor, he felt constrained to take his name, and vowed to carry out his design for renewing the church.

Shortly after settling into the Vatican, the Polish Holy Father was faced with the problem of the Puebla, Mexico, meeting of Latin American bishops scheduled for the fall of 1978. Twice postponed because of the deaths of Paul VI and John Paul I, this important follow-up of the Medellín conference, ten years earlier, had become the object of dissension among the bishops of that vast continent and Vatican officialdom. In the text prepared for discussion of the church's involvement in the social, economic, and political problems of the Latin American countries, a minority of cardinals and bishops felt that too much stress was being placed on the secular activities of priests, nuns, and lay apostles, and not enough attention was being paid to the more spiritual aspects of the Christian message. This was the opinion of the auxiliary bishop of Bogotá, Msgr. Alfonso López Trujillo, who, as secretary of CELAM (the Conference of Latin American Bishops), was in charge of the final arrangements for the meeting and its agenda.

Abetted by the curial cardinal, Sebastiano Baggio, and the controversial Jesuit activist, Roger Vekemans, Bishop Trujillo felt that the apostles of "liberation theology" were too greatly influenced by Communist ideology in their interpretation of the Gospels. They seemed to advocate a revolutionary approach to problems resulting from the exploitation of the poor by the rich landowners, industrial financiers, and international bankers who supported right-wing and dictatorial governments in these lands.

Trujillo's policies were opposed by Cardinals Raul Silva Henriquez of Chile, Juan Landazuri Ricketts of Peru, Aloisio Lorscheider of Brazil, and a large number of other prelates, from Dom Heldar Pessoa Camara of Recife to Archbishop Oscar Romero of San Salvador.

As cardinal of Krakow, Carol Wojtyla had been aware of the dispute between the two Latin American factions. Now, as pope, he had to confront the situation with a workable solution.

83

Evidently, from the beginning of his pontificate John Paul had made up his mind to imitate his predecessor, Paul VI, who had presided over the opening of the Medellín Conference in Bogotá in 1968. Hence, despite the opposition of Cardinal Baggio and several curial officials, John Paul set the date for the Puebla meeting as the last week in January 1979. He then made plans to fly to that great land where the church had first taken root in the New World. Behind the pontiff's decision was a desire to see for himself the extremes of poverty troubling its largely Catholic population. Then, like a new St. Paul the Apostle, he hoped to provide a personal, charismatic encouragement to the people in a Christian confrontation of their problems.

Pope John Paul left Rome in a giant Alitalia plane specially fitted for papal travel on January 24, and made his first stop at Santo Domingo. He was given a jubilant welcome by the Dominican Republic's President Antonio Guzman and his wife, along with the nation's cardinal, Octavio Beras. Well over 250,000 people lined the streets from the airport to the Plaza de Independencia, where the pontiff said mass in the public square. Later, he visited the tomb of Christopher Columbus in the ancient cathedral and addressed priests, nuns, students, and the whole Catholic people.

After a night in the papal nuncio's palace, he left for Mexico City the following morning. There, in the capital's municipal airport, he was given a warm but brief welcome by President and Mrs. Jose Lopez Portillo and then handed over to the church authorities. Close to half a million people greeted him during his journey to the nation's venerable cathedral. The pontiff then said a public mass and visited with Archbishop Ernesto Corripio Ahumada, the clergy and nuns, the Polish colony, and diplomats.

John Paul spent two days in this ancient center of Aztec and Christian culture. He made a special pilgrimage to the Shrine of our Lady of Guadalupe, where in 1531 the Virgin Mary appeared to an Indian peasant, instructing him to have the bishop erect a basilica on the spot in her honor.

Then the pope was off in a specially mounted vehicle

over the mountains to Puebla de los Angeles, an ancient fortress town that now harbored a modern city as well as the vestiges of a once-flourishing Catholicism in its numerous churches.

In his inaugural talk, delivered to the continent's bishops assembled in the spacious, remodeled, seventeenth-century Palafox Seminary, the pope gave a long and intricate resume of the problems confronting the Latin American church, together with suggested solutions. He proposed a radical Christian ordering of the socioeconomic systems that would bring about justice in government and tranquility to the people. In discussing the church's part in this transformation, the pope insisted that while Jesus Christ had condemned the rapacity of the leaders of his time, he had not been a revolutionary advocating the overthrow of the colonial system. John Paul thus advised priests, nuns, and missionaries that they were not to get directly involved in political movements.

That statement caused considerable anguish and confusion among his listeners, many of whom were nuns and clerics deeply involved with their people in the battle for a decent livelihood, land, homes, and the education of their children—all necessities being denied them precisely by the political systems under which they lived. They feared, rightly, that the papal statement could easily be used by intransigent rightists to terrorize any cleric or committed Christian working with the people for social and economic justice.

Reacting to the strong criticism that immediately appeared in the press, the pope, while at Oaxaca visiting the Indian peasants in an impoverished mountain area, took a strong stand against the exploitation of these peasants, promising to aid them by being the "voice of the voiceless."

During the following days, as he traveled in and about Guadalajara and Monterey, the pope was greeted with jubilant festivities. In his talks, John Paul repeated his support for the poverty-stricken. He lashed out against their oppressors while encouraging priests, nuns, and laypeople to live out their lives in a renewed Christian fashion. Everywhere

An international group of economists also met to discuss issues of the CELAM conference.

The pope arrived by helicopter in the Indian village of Cuilapan de Guerrero outside the city of Oaxaca, Mexico. Later he ordained ten Indians as priests.

A major stop in the pope's visit to his native Poland was the monastery of Jasna Gora with its famed shrine of Our Lady of Czestochowa.

During motorcades among the jubilant Polish throngs, the pope rode in a "popemobile."

he went he made a valiant attempt to elude his protective guards. He moved among the crowds, being jostled, lifting up children to admire and kiss, and making direct contact with whoever could get near him.

Departing Mexico late on the evening of January 29, the Holy Father made a stop at Nassau, where he was greeted at midnight by more than a hundred thousand people assembled in the sports arena. It was a tired but exhilarated Holy Father who flew back to Rome that morning. A week after his return, he acknowledged the validity of liberation theology in a public audience describing this expression of the Christian message as being in keeping with Christ's words and actions.

A short time later, the Polish pope put the finishing touches on a long, rambling meditation, the "Redeemer of Man," published in March as his first encyclical. Written by hand in Polish at short intervals, it differed considerably from previous papal documents. It was an exhortation attempting to touch all the bases of Christian consciousness in the contemporary world. It pointed the church toward a "new advent" in preparation for the year A.D. 2000.

The pope said that Christianity had to adopt a new way of understanding itself and the world. He reassured those who showed a lack of courage in pursuing movements toward the reunion of the Christian churches. All in all the document, though long and intricate, seemed to exude the courage and enthusiasm that characterized the new pontiff in his earliest activities.

John Paul took quickly to travel by helicopter, flying back and forth across Italy from Assisi to Naples and from the birthplace of his predecessor, John Paul I, in the mountains near Venice to Monte Cassino. He made frequent pastoral visitations to the parishes of Rome and thought nothing of flying down to Castel Gandolfo for a few hours of quiet and a swim in the olympic-sized pool he had installed with the remark that it was cheaper than another conclave.

Plans for a papal visit to Poland had been broached in

the press from almost the moment of his election. In a conversation with the Polish president, Henryk Jablonski, in attendance at the pope's installation as bishop of Rome, John Paul was told he would be warmly welcomed by the Communist government as the head of the State of Vatican City and as a famous native son. Despite considerable speculation regarding a possibly unhappy reaction in the Kremlin and the Polish Politburo to a Pole as pope, there was no indication of concern on the part of the Soviet rulers. John Paul had actually received the Soviet foreign minister, Andrei Gromyko, in audience in January—it was his sixth visit to the Vatican—for a long conversation.

A compromise was eventually worked out between the government and the Polish primate, Cardinal Wyszynsky. The date of the papal visit was set for early June, covering the feast of Pentecost rather than the anniversary of the murder of St. Stanislaw of Krakow in May 1079. That prelate had been killed by King Boleslaw the Bold; the church canonized the archbishop as a martyr, while the Communists labeled him a rebel. Both the nation and the church then cooperated in massive preparations for the papal visit with its outdoor celebrations of the Liturgy and papal visits to churches and shrines in Warsaw, Krakow, his native Wadowice, and the surrounding mountainous areas.

Arriving in Warsaw's military airport promptly at 10:00 A.M. on June 2, 1979, John Paul kissed the ground before receiving an emotional welcome from his former colleague and mentor, the aging Cardinal Wyszynsky. This was followed by a formal salute from the Polish governmental authorities. Jubilant crowds, estimated in the millions, greeted the pope as his motorcade made its slow way into the center of the city. The people sang native religious and national songs and tossed flowers in his path. After a visit to St. John's Cathedral and lunch with the cardinal, John Paul was driven to the Belvedere Palace, where he had a prolonged colloquium with Polish governmental officials. He assured them that his visit was purely a spiritual pilgrimage and that the church asked nothing of the government other than the freedom to carry out its functions.

The pope spoke to crowds outside his residence in Krakow, the city he left when elected to the Chair of St. Peter. On the following two pages are paintings from the papal visit to the death camps at Auschwitz and Birkenau, now memorials to the millions of people killed there by the Nazis.

90

The pope's visit to the United States began in
Boston.

A short time later John Paul mounted the stairs to a magnificently severe altar on a large platform facing the Tomb of the Unknown Soldier in Victory Square. There he celebrated a papal mass, the first ever in a Communist country. Calling himself "a pilgrim pope," he said that he was going to give witness to the fact that "Jesus Christ could not be kept out of the history of man in any part of the globe." With more than three hundred thousand people crowded into the area around the square, the Polish authorities had wisely arranged for order to be kept by church ushers, with the local police out of sight. There were no incidents.

The next morning, Pentecost Sunday, the pontiff celebrated a liturgy for youth in Castle Square outside St. Anne's Church. He encouraged his innumerable audience to remain true to the Cross of Christ, whose symbol they were carrying. In Gniezno that same afternoon, he repeated the Mass of Pentecost in the ancient cathedral of this primatial see. In the course of his homily he recognized a banner carried by a contingent of Czech pilgrims and cried out that as the Slavic pope he would give special witness to the faith of Eastern Europe. In several talks thereafter he discussed the Christianization of this part of the world during the early Middle Ages and encouraged his listeners to be proud of their great heritage.

On Monday morning John Paul arrived in Czestochowa by helicopter. He was greeted by nearly four hundred thousand people from all over Poland assembled at the Shrine of the Black Madonna. Besides celebrating a solemn three-hour mass, he spent the next two days in and about the famous monastery of Jasna Gora and held a consultation with the Polish bishops gathered for their annual meeting.

The pope spoke of normalizing relations between church and state. Then, in an open-air address to a contingent of Silesian miners with their wives, who were dressed in native costumes with bright red bandannas on their heads, the Holy Father insisted that "work is a fundamental factor of man's existence." It was not, however, the *raison d'être* of his being, as the Marxists claimed.

95

In Krakow, in his hometown of Wadowice, and in Auschwitz, during the homily at his masses, he spoke out loudly about the relations between religion and politics. Finally, at Birkenau, where the worst of the massacres of Jews and Christians had taken place, he referred to this contemporary horror as "the Golgotha of the modern world."

Everywhere he turned in his incessant contact with literally millions of people, the pope's gestures and facial expressions, his habit of admiring and embracing children, and the figure he presented with his arms outstretched as if in a great embrace of all the people, exhibited a charm that could only be interpreted as a spark of holiness in action.

Even when, on his home territory of Nowy Targ in the Tatra Mountains, he brought up the seamier side of Polish life—the drunkenness, broken marriages, violated vocations —his message was received with awe.

He spent the last part of his nine-day visit in and about Krakow. He presided at the closing session of a diocesan synod he had started in 1972, visited old haunts, and encouraged both the youth and the older generation to speak up courageously in support of their Polish traditions and proudly hand them on unspoiled to the next generation. After kneeling down to kiss the ground at the airport before his departure for Rome, he disappeared, a tired but triumphant pontiff who had just confronted the Communist world and found it vulnerable.

John Paul's visit to Poland had no immediate political effect, either in stirring rebellious sentiments among oppressed people or in antagonizing the Communist system. Quite sensibly, the Politburo in the Kremlin as well as in Warsaw accepted the inevitable by playing along with the papal visit.

Just how deep a spiritual rejuvenation the papal presence had enkindled was impossible to say. The visit had certainly given Polish Catholics the feeling that God was very close to them—a tremendous consolation in their struggle to preserve the faith of the coming generation. An honest Communist commentator admitted that even he had been

Mass on the Boston Common was celebrated in the rain.

96

impressed by what he would have termed in his youth "an act of God." Although now he knew better, "the old belief still retained a haunting quality."

On his return to Rome, John Paul spent several days resting and refreshing his energies at Castel Gandolfo, slowly turning his attention to Vatican affairs. In early June, he announced his first batch of new cardinals, which included his own and his predecessor's successors in Krakow and in Venice; the archbishops of Armagh in Ireland, Turin in Italy, Toronto in Canada, Nagasaki in Japan; and four curial officials, Ladislaw Rubin, his Polish confidante, archbishops Caprio and Civardi of the papal household, and Agostino Casaroli, whom he had named to replace the recently deceased French cardinal, Jean Villot, as secretary of state. Casaroli's selection was well received, particularly by the Communist world, for he had been the genius behind the Ostpolitik of Popes John and Paul.

Turning his attention to world politics, the Holy Father studied the urgent request he had received from Kurt Waldheim of the United Nations that he address the General Assembly on the anniversary of Pope Paul's visit on October 4, 1965. When word spread of the papal trip to New York, the Irish bishops made a bid for a stopover in the Emerald Isle, and almost every city and town in the United States and Canada sent invitations for him to visit them. To the suppressed dissatisfaction of his original host, who wanted the Pope to make the United Nations encounter the immediate goal and high point of his papal itinerary, John Paul decided to accept the Irish invitation, then fly to New York via Boston; and finally flesh out his journey with stopovers in Philadelphia, Des Moines, Chicago, and Washington, D.C.

Preceded by an exploratory, decision-making tour by Bishop Paul Marcinkus, the pope's visit to Ireland and the United States was a series of sensational experiences covered totally by local and national television. There were open-air masses in each of the cities that hosted him.

In Dublin and Drogheda, in Limerick and Knock, the Irish people were simply overwhelmed by this astute

St. Patrick's Cathedral, New York City.

Pope John Paul II greeted members of the international community in the garden of the United Nations.

98

Crowds waited for the papal motorcade to arrive in Harlem in New York City.

Pope John Paul II addressed the General Assembly of the United Nations.

charmer whose thespian experience as a young man had taught him how to mesmerize a crowd. Even when in the course of his sermons he warned the chronically poor Irish people against the ravages of consumerism and the deadening influence of materialism, he was greeted with total love. And while his appeal to terrorist extremists was shrugged off with contempt, the papal presence in Ireland was compared to the original implanting of the faith by St. Patrick. It would quickly become part of a heritage that would be woven into the Irish world of legend.

In Boston, John Paul was assured by Rosalynn Carter that America welcomed him with love. And while the weather treated him with some disdain—his mass on Boston's Copley Square and visit to the Battery and Shea Stadium in New York were punctuated with downpours— the citizenry reflected the First Lady's sentiments.

In his talk before the United Nations on October 2, the pope made an eloquent plea for an authentic effort at achieving world peace. He touched on several delicate areas of discord and condemned the very concept of the arms race in this day and age. "Is this the heritage this generation of statesmen wants to hand on to its children?" he asked with righteous vehemence. Putting himself at the disposal of the secretary general, he patiently greeted the staff and personnel of this vast organization. Then he joined Cardinal Cook at St. Patrick's Cathedral and journeyed through the slum areas of Harlem and the Bronx on his way to celebrate a late evening mass at Yankee Stadium. The next morning in Madison Square Garden, he charmed some twenty thousand youth, who entertained him with songs and pantomimes, to which he responded in kind.

In Philadelphia, Des Moines, and Chicago, John Paul visited local shrines and establishments before celebrating a public mass for vast aggregates of people. In the Windy City he addressed a gathering of the American hierarchy, citing his own experiences as a pastor before laying down the law as to the church's moral teaching on abortion, birth control, the sanctity of marriage, divorce, and homosexuality. This

101

was a theme he had mentioned somewhat less vehemently in Philadelphia and was to repeat unabashedly in Washington. The reaction was immediate and perplexed.

While no one expected the pope to change church teaching on these matters, most observers felt that he could have adopted a more benevolent attitude toward the people whose lives were being affected by these evils. It was particularly in view of his insistence in "Redeemer of Man" on the total extension of Christ's salvific life and death to the whole of mankind, saints and sinners equally, that his apparent lack of compassion seemed so incongruous. In a sense he seemed to be destroying with his discourse the great spiritual rapport he had achieved with the mesmeric quality of his presence.

In his Saturday afternoon at Jimmy Carter's White House, not only did he lay to rest the ghost of two hundred years of anti-Catholic no-popery, but he had an obviously cordial lunch and visit with the president and his family. After that, under presidential guidance, he greeted a large gathering of the nation's elite, from statesmen to politicians and policemen gathered on the White House grounds.

In the National Shrine, on the property of the Catholic University of America the next morning, he met with a group of students who had held an all-night vigil. He jokingly assured them that while they prayed, he had slept very well indeed. On entering the vast church, he received the only confrontation of his journey when Sr. Mary Theresa Kane, representing the nation's nuns, told him of the unhappiness visited on millions of women by their lack of equality with men within the church. Unaware of the implications of her observations, the pope received her kindly, but in a prepared speech he insisted that as the Blessed Virgin Mary had not formed part of the apostolic hierarchy in the primitive church, the chance for women to play a part in the priestly ministry was nil.

In his address to the academic convocation of the university, he seemed to go out of his way to praise the activities of the church's theologians, encouraging them to serve

The pope greeted Chicago Catholic nuns and priests in Holy Name Cathedral.

the church with proper freedom. That afternoon he celebrated a final mass on the mall in the nation's capitol and then departed from Andrews Air Force base for Rome and home.

While John Paul had left the impression behind him of a truly accommodating Holy Father, there was also a feeling that all was not totally well with his prosecution of the reforms authorized by John and Paul's council.

During a quick, impromptu visit to Turkey for the Feast of St. Andrew, he and the Orthodox patriarch, Demetrios, assisted at each other's Liturgy without, however, participating in the reception of the Eucharist. Then John Paul settled into a round of Vatican chores. These included presiding over a synod of Dutch bishops in Rome, which attempted to reestablish harmony in that troubled church. He called for a similar synod of the Ukrainian church under his guidance to resolve hierarchical conflicts due to the patriarchal ambitions of the confessor of the faith, Cardinal Josef Slipyi.

The pope also sanctioned the *ancien* Holy Office's interrogation of the Dutch theologian, Edward Schillebeeckx, and its censure of the Swiss professor at the University of Tübingen in Germany, Hans Küng. Both of these theologians were charged with watering down the church's ancient belief in the divinity of Jesus Christ. While Schillebeeckx had the backing of his cardinal, Johannes Willebrands, Küng's troubles stemmed in good part from his defiance of the old Holy Office and his attack on papal infallibility. Nevertheless, when the papal censure came, depriving him of his title as a Catholic theologian, Küng submitted. Publicly asserting his loyalty to pope and church and supported by theologians and churchmen of all persuasions, Küng surrendered his Catholic professorial standing but was retained on the university staff as head of the Institute of Ecumenical Research, of which he was the founder.

Pope John Paul's concern with the particularities of Catholic belief and practice crept out once more in his long sermon on the Eucharist on Holy Thursday. In addition to

Papal mass in Grant Park, Chicago.

elucidating the magnificent mystery repeated in the Sacrament of the Lord's Supper, the pope indulged in a series of cautions regarding the celebration of the Liturgy and the significance of the Mass as a sacrifice as well as a eucharistic re-presentation of the Last Supper. He called for an end to ritual experimentation and a return to a reverential approach to the reception and reservation of the Blessed Sacrament. These concerns were fully in keeping with his frequent reminders to monks, priests, and nuns about the sacred character of their calling and his desire that they should return to a more traditional practice of religious piety and unworldly dress.

Nevertheless, John Paul also is concerned with the church universal, where there are innumerable and great activities—the *magnalia Dei*—upon which he can bestow an encouraging benediction. Everywhere in the vast expanse covered by the church, dedicated Christians are intent on making the presence of Christ, the Redeemer of Man, felt in the contemporary world. In the universities and the *comunidades de base,* among the rich and the extremely poor, in the great slum areas of the large cities of the First and Third Worlds as well as among the proletariat under Communist domination, Catholics and Christians of every age, race, and color are striving to put into effect the basic tenets of the Gospel.

In keeping with his inaugural promise that he would open a new path in history, John Paul continues his worldwide pilgrimages. His visit to Africa in May 1980 was to a church burgeoning in former colonial territories, the now-independent nations of Zaire, Congo-Brazzaville, Kenya, Ghana, Upper Volta, and Ivory Coast. He talked with their three native cardinals—Otunga, Malula, and Zoungrana—and saw swiftly growing seminaries, schools, and catechetical and ecumenical programs supported by people inordinately proud of their parishes and local priests, nuns, and brothers.

In July the Holy Father departed for Brazil, where he sought to unite the various factions in the church caught

On the following three pages, paintings depict Pope John Paul II celebrating mass on the Mall in Washington, D.C., and meeting invited guests with President Jimmy Carter outside the White House.

between the apostles of social justice struggling against economic and political exploitation on the one hand, and, on the other, the proponents of law and order. Also of concern is the revival of vast, indigenous superstitions, and the evils of genocide, governmental repression, and terrorism. Received with massive demonstrations of affection and love everywhere he turned, John Paul brought back to Rome a new sense of the papal apostolate. He said his hope was "to contribute to the growth of the Christian faith in these regions that are already ripe for the harvest . . . while encouraging all the peoples to work for human progress at the service of brotherhood and peace."

V
This Church, These Times

The Watts section of Los Angeles.

In the twenty years separating the pontificate of Pope John XXIII from that of John Paul II, the Catholic church underwent a series of internal revolutions the likes of which had not been experienced since the Protestant Reformation and the Catholic reaction of the sixteenth century. Recalling the upheavals following the Council of Trent (1545–1563), the secretary of state, Cardinal Tardini, had advised Pope John against calling Vatican Council II into being. He failed. And the church has been in a state of turmoil ever since.

John inaugurated the council on October 11, 1962. Three years later, on December 8, 1965, his successor, Paul VI, brought that assembly to a successful close. In between, the Catholic church subjected itself to a thorough examination of conscience. The council produced sixteen documents whose implications were sufficient to literally turn the church upside down.

The church John had set out to rejuvenate is still reverberating with doctrinal and disciplinary implosions; it is still striving to catch up with the "signs of the times." It is not

113

certain that John would have been happy with some of the developments within the postconciliar church. But he did possess the virtue of equanimity and would have taken the exodus of priests and nuns from the active ministry, the drop in church attendance, and other disaffections with sadness but with understanding.

In the fifteen years of his pontificate, Pope Paul VI tried to keep a firm hand on the developments within the church, frequently without success. He had been a champion of change, but at a slower pace and in a lower key than radical Christians desired. He did revamp much of the church's administrative organization at the top; he encouraged the bishops' participation in overall policymaking at the center; and he legitimized structural and disciplinary changes in dealing with marriage, the liturgy, and clerical life. His successor, John Paul I, abolished the pomp and ceremony surrounding the papacy as a political organization, then suddenly vanished into eternity.

The next Holy Father, John Paul II, had solid reasons for rejoicing as he gazed across the world from his study high in the papal palace on the second anniversary of his election as bishop of Rome. Despite the horrors of terrorism and fratricidal warfare, the exploitation of the poor and the breakdown of moral values affecting his flock and his world, the pope could see that the Catholic church had never been in a better position to carry out its original mission—to preach the Gospel to every creature.

During his first two years as pope, John Paul II obviously imitated the determination of both Saints Peter and Paul to give personal witness to the presence of Christ everywhere in the world. The Holy Father, "in journeyings often," crisscrossed the globe from Mexico and the United States in the New World, to Italy, Ireland, Poland, and France in the Old, and on to Africa and Brazil in the Southern Hemisphere. Received with tumultuous enthusiasm everywhere he turned, John Paul left the impression of a man of tremendous strength and religious vitality who was

An ecumenical youth group meeting in Wisconsin.

determined to uplift mankind to new heights of spiritual awareness.

While adhering to the early church's conviction that it was "in but not of" this world, the majority of Catholics were seriously involved with the issues troubling contemporary society. On each continent, in each nation, Catholic lay men and women were gathering together not merely for liturgical functions, but also in concerned groups to discuss the tasks immediately affecting their lives and those of their compatriots. Their worries ran from the involvement of youth with drugs and pornography to the breakdown of family cohesion and the evils of political oppression. Nor was their attention ever diverted from the need for reform within the church's structure and the manner in which the church said its prayers.

The close involvement of the laity in guiding the church's destiny had been set out in the two principal documents of the council—the "Dogmatic Constitution on the Church" and the "Pastoral Constitution on the Church." The implementation of these directives resulted in the formation of lay committees on the parochial, diocesan, and national levels. In 1967 these organizations exploded into a series of international meetings in Rome, the most significant of which was that of the Lay Apostolate. So vociferous did this gathering become that Pope Paul VI felt obliged to advise its organizers that they were not to create a hierarchy of the laity in opposition to that of the pope and clergy.

While the papal alarm was exaggerated, it recognized that the baptized Christian actually constituted the body of Christ, and as such, both clerics and faithful had to be involved in guiding the church's life. Actually, from the second session of the council onward, Catholic lay men and women served as official observers and participated in preparing many of the conciliar documents. At that assembly's close, a number were brought into the Vatican offices as consultors and as officials in the secretariats for the Laity and for Justice and Peace. Then, in pastoral councils and synods around the world, the laity gave witness to the vitality of their faith and

A group of Catholic lay people meet in Rome.

116

Dorothy Day of the Catholic Worker movement.

Grape pickers, led by Cesar Chavez's United Farm Workers, strike for better working conditions in the vineyards near Delano, California.

the seriousness of their commitment to making Jesus Christ present in the everyday affairs of their community, parish, and nation.

Throughout the world, a heroic attempt was made to help people help themselves by setting up small units known as *comunidades de base.* These units consisted mainly of poor families dedicated to their spiritual, educational, and material uplift. Guided by priests, nuns, and lay apostles, these people read the New Testament in the light of their social and political situation, seeking the courage and inspiration to achieve the dignity proper to their status as human beings.

In his pilgrimages to five continents, Pope Paul VI visited the poor in their slums and hovels, bringing them hope and consolation. Then, in his encyclical "Development of Peoples" of 1967 and his "Call to Action" of 1971, he accurately described their situation before demanding a total change in the world's political and economic systems that would eliminate such conditions. While the papal admonitions fell on deaf ears among the mighty and the wealthy, they were taken to heart by many church and lay leaders, particularly in the oppressed portions of the globe.

Little by little bishops and clergy became involved in the movements for justice and human dignity that had been so highly lauded by the council and in papal directives.

In his visits to both the Old and the New World, Pope John Paul II emphasized the church's total involvement in the struggle for human rights, reaching out especially to the youth. In Rome, he held weekly meetings with crowds of young people prior to his regular audiences, giving encouragement to their numberless organizations—from university movements and scouting to sports and unions of young workers.

The comment to Pope John Paul by Sr. Theresa Kane during his visit to the National Shrine of the Immaculate Conception in Washington touched off a minor controversy regarding the role of women—particularly of nuns—in the church's activities. This event highlighted the tremendous

119

part played by women, despite their lack of priestly ordination, down through the ages in the development of the church. Today, without both religious and lay women, the church would cease to function. The Holy Father practically admitted this as he sought to offset a movement in favor of the ordination of women by pointing out the part played by Mary and the other New Testament women disciples.

The universal character of the church in the twentieth century had been reemphasized by recent popes. In expanding the college of cardinals so that there would be a prince of the church in all the major sees around the world, Pope John gave special attention to that universality. In 1946 Pius XII had given Peking its first native cardinal; in 1960 John had created the first Japanese cardinal, Peter Tatsuo Doi of Tokyo—though the Japanese church was but a miniscule element in that nation's teeming millions. It was not, however, an unimportant factor in Japanese life, with its Catholic university of Sancta Sophia and its bookshops and information centers serving as a point of contact for the cultures of the East and West.

Throughout the Far East, a great missionary effort was in progress despite political and ideological obstacles. In India, where Catholics were but one or two percent of the population, there were cardinals in Bombay and Calcutta, a full-fledged hierarchy, and growing numbers of native priests and religious caring for an exceptionally devout people. The Indian church made progress in adapting the liturgy to Oriental expression—not hesitating to introduce eastern dance patterns into the church's rites and ceremonies.

Despite the paucity of a Catholic constituency, there was a cardinal in Karachi, Pakistan. The church was represented in the primarily Moslem nations of Iraq, Iran, and Afghanistan, as well as in the Arabian Peninsula, by small groups, mainly foreigners, who provided educational and medical services and who were encouraged by apostolic delegates.

There were cardinals in Seoul and Hanoi despite the great difficulties with ideological oppression in Indochina and the totalitarian nature of the government of South Korea. In

Sister Theresa Kane, president of the Leadership Conference of Women Religious.

An ecumenical panel of American women discusses racial prejudice and its effect on their lives.

120

McMillan
Bombay, India

Roman Catholics in India interpret Christian teachings through Hindu dances, an indigenization of the liturgy.

the Philippines, a largely Catholic nation, the cardinal of Manila was at odds with the oppressive Marcos government; Indonesia had its prince of the church in the cardinal of Jakarta. So did the chain of islands running down through Samoa, with the native bishop of Apia, Cardinal Pio Taofinu'u.

Not only was the church holding its own in Australia and New Zealand, but continental China was beginning to loosen the impenetrable "bamboo curtain," allowing some of the three million Christians who had gone underground during Mao's revolution to surface. In 1979 the Jesuits were welcomed back to Shanghai to reopen their Aurora University and medical school. And in 1980, two cardinals, Roger Etchegaray of Marseilles and Franz Koenig of Vienna, were invited to visit the mainland. Gradually the Vatican was encouraged to seek a way to recognize the Patriotic Catholic Association with its locally elected bishops without offending the thousands of Catholics whose total loyalty to the Holy See had caused them grave deprivation and persecution.

While the churches under Russian domination in Eastern Europe suffered great hardship, the loyalty of a hard core of practicing Catholics—from Lithuania and Poland to Hungary and Czechoslovakia—could not be shaken. Thus, the Vatican was able to restore the hierarchy in all these nations, even exchanging diplomatic representatives with Yugoslavia. Despite the opposition of exiled Russian Catholics, the Holy See was in ecumenical contact with the patriarch of Moscow and the orthodox hierarchy.

Throughout Central and Latin America, Catholics were thoroughly involved in the political and economic crises that kept these lands in continual turmoil. Amid their all but insurmountable difficulties, one thing was certain: the church, with the majority of its bishops, priests, nuns, and lay apostles, simply could not abstract itself from local and national conflicts even if those conflicts involved a rebellion against exploitation by governments and monopolistic financial interests. Whether for or against the "liberation theology" that characterized Latin American rebellion against oppression,

123

the church leaders could not escape the continent's material and social problems.

In Africa, the church continued to experience its greatest expansion despite the turbulence affecting each new nation as it strove to achieve full political and economic independence. After World War II, a great wave of anticolonialism resulted in the formation of some thirty independent nations, most of which immediately sought diplomatic exchanges with the Vatican. At the same time, the church was forced to prepare an indigenous clergy capable of conducting the spiritual governance of its dioceses and parishes. With the creation of a native cardinal in Tanzania by Pope John in 1960, the African church came of age; it now has eight princes of the church scattered over the continent.

In most respects the churches in the United States and Canada were thriving, though the numbers of vocations to the priesthood and religious life had dramatically lessened. Nevertheless, lay involvement in theology, social and religious concerns, liturgical renewal, and diocesan and parochial affairs had never been more intense or more effective. Concern about schools, catechetical programs, abortion, divorce, teenage problems, and the political and economic situation were debated with considerable acrimony by traditionalist and progressive Catholics. But this was a sign of life and growth.

In the overall picture, the enormous effort of most Catholics to follow the conciliar line had by 1980 begun to produce positive results throughout the church. A new spirit was detectable in local efforts to reach the young while at the same time caring for the needs of middle-aged and older Catholics, many of whom felt disoriented by changes in the liturgy, the church's new rules for devotion and discipline, and a revised approach to moral and social values.

The phenomena of the postconciliar church varied greatly in different parts of the world. But as Pope John Paul's journeys demonstrated, there was no way of avoiding the presence in the contemporary world of This Church in These Times.

Children leave a special mass said for them at Our Lady of Sorrows Church in Chicago.

124